a

simple

life-changing **prayer**

a

simple

life-changing **prayer**

Discovering the Power of St. Ignatius Loyola's Examen

JIM MANNEY

LOYOLAPRESS.
A JESUIT MINISTRY
Chicago

LOYOLA PRESS.
A JESUIT MINISTRY

3441 N. Ashland Avenue
Chicago, Illinois 60657
(800) 621-1008
www.loyolapress.com

Quotes from *The Spiritual Exercises* are from *The Spiritual Exercises of St. Ignatius*, translated by Louis J. Puhl (Chicago: Loyola Press, 1951). Used by permission.

Scripture excerpts are from the *New American Bible* with Revised New Testament and Psalms Copyright © 1991, 1986, 1970 Confraternity of Christian Doctrine, Inc., Washington, DC. Used with permission. All rights reserved. No portion of the *New American Bible* may be reprinted without permission in writing from the copyright holder.

Cover image: PhotoAlto/Frederic Cirou/Getty Images

Library of Congress Cataloging-in-Publication Data
Manney, Jim.
  A simple, life-changing prayer : discovering the power of St. Ignatius Loyola's Examen / Jim Manney.
    p. cm.
  ISBN-13: 978-0-8294-3535-1
  ISBN-10: 0-8294-3535-2
  1. Ignatius, of Loyola, Saint, 1491–1556. Exercitia spiritualia. 2. Prayer—Catholic Church. 3. Spiritual life—Catholic Church. I. Title.
  BX2179.L8M327 2011
  248.3--dc22

2010044933

Printed in the United States of America
20 21 22 23 Versa 14 13 12 11 10 9

contents

preface

The *examen* changed everything for me, but that almost didn't happen. For years I had occasionally heard people talk about the examen as a good way to pray. I went to a Jesuit college; I remember one of my teachers saying that St. Ignatius of Loyola himself thought that the examen was *the* indispensible prayer. But I wasn't interested because I thought they were talking about the Examination of Conscience.

The Examination of Conscience was the methodical inventory of sins that I was taught to do as a boy in Catholic schools of the 1960s. I would work my way through lists of faults, toting up my offenses in preparation for the sacrament of confession. This was a grim exercise, also a confusing one. I understood lying, and eventually I knew what lust was. But what was "acedia?" (It means spiritual laziness.) At any rate, the charm of the Examination of Conscience wore off as I grew older. I set it aside and moved on to other things, not all of them improvements. When people talked about the examen, this is what I thought they meant, and I wasn't interested. I thought it was just the thing for people who like that kind of thing, but I wasn't one of them.

Then I learned that the Ignatian examen was *not* the old, depressing Examination of Conscience. Quite the opposite. This was a prayer that focused on God's presence in the real world. It looked to a God who was near to me, present in my world, and active in my life. It told me to approach prayer with gratitude, not guilt. It helped me find God in my life as I lived it, not in some heavenly realm beyond space and time. The examen had me take myself seriously, as I was, not as I wished I was or thought I could be someday if I worked hard enough.

It's no exaggeration to say that the examen changed everything. It might change things for you too.

the examen in a nutshell

I don't know exactly what a prayer is.
I do know how to pay attention.
—Mary Oliver, "The Summer Day"

The *examen* is a method of reviewing your day in the presence of God. It's actually an attitude more than a method, a time set aside for thankful reflection on where God is in your everyday life. It has five steps, which most people take more or less in order, and it usually takes 15 to 20 minutes per day. Here it is in a nutshell:

1. **Ask God for light.**
   I want to look at my day with God's eyes, not merely my own.
2. **Give thanks.**
   The day I have just lived is a gift from God. Be grateful for it.
3. **Review the day.**
   I carefully look back on the day just completed, being guided by the Holy Spirit.
4. **Face your shortcomings.**
   I face up to what is wrong—in my life and in me.
5. **Look toward the day to come.**
   I ask where I need God in the day to come.

Simple? Yes. Easy? Not really. Sometimes praying the examen is smooth and joyful; sometimes it's arduous. If the examen prayer is doing its job, it will bring up painful moments and cause you to look at behavior that's embarrassing. Sometimes you squirm praying the examen, but why would you have it otherwise? Real prayer is about change, and change is never easy.

But there's nothing complicated or mysterious about making the examen part of your life. The subject matter of the examen *is* your life—specifically the day you have just lived through. The examen looks for signs of God's presence in the events of the day: lunch with a friend, a walk in the park, a kind word from a colleague, a challenge met, a duty discharged. The examen likes the humdrum. God is present in transcendent "spiritual" moments, but he's also there when you cook dinner, write a memo, answer email, and run errands. The examen looks at your conscious experience. The ebb and flow of your moods and feelings are full of spiritual meaning. Nothing is so trivial that it's meaningless. What do you think about while sitting in traffic or waiting in a long line at the grocery store? What's your frame of mind while doing boring and repetitive chores? You'll be surprised at how significant such moments can be when you really look at them.

The examen surprised me because it was so unlike prayer as I had previously understood it. Prayer for me was a time set apart. With the examen the boundaries between prayer and life became blurred. People usually pray the daily examen at a set time (for me usually in the morning), but there's no reason why we can't pray the examen while standing in that long line at the grocery store. After all, God is there too.

But in another way the examen didn't surprise me at all. God is certainly there while you're standing in line. All you need to pray the examen is a little quiet time. This made intuitive sense. I am God's creature living in God's world; *of course* God would be present in my everyday experience. If prayer is making a connection with God, it makes perfect sense to spend some time finding God in my conscious experience of daily life.

In fact, the examen is a very old practice. The word *examen* comes from a Latin word that means both an examination and the act of weighing or judging something. It's as old as Socrates's instruction to "know thyself." A practice of regular self-scrutiny is found in most religions of the world, and this is certainly the case with Christianity. To follow the path of Jesus, we must regularly scrutinize our behavior and ask how closely our actions conform to Christ's.

Five hundred years ago, St. Ignatius of Loyola made an innovative twist on this ancient tradition of prayerful reflection. He made it a way to experience God as well as to assess our behavior. Ignatius's famous book *The Spiritual Exercises* is a guide to an intense experience of conversion to the cause of Christ. He designed the daily examen to sustain and extend this experience. Ignatius wanted to help people develop a reflective habit of mind that is constantly attuned to God's presence and responsive to God's leading. The examen became the foundation for this graced awareness. Ignatius wanted Jesuits to practice the examen twice a day—at noon and before sleep. He considered it so important that he insisted that Jesuits pray the examen even when they were too busy to pray in other ways.

Over the centuries, the practice of the Ignatian examen has taken on different forms. For a long time it closely resembled the Examination of Conscience that troubled the prayer of my youth. In recent decades Jesuits have been restoring the examen to something more closely resembling Ignatius's original vision for a prayer practice that would help us find God in our everyday lives and respond more generously to his gifts and blessings. That's the form of the examen that's presented in this book.

I've read everything about the examen that I could find. Interestingly, there's not a lot written about it. Except for a couple of small books and a few learned essays, most of what I found has been pamphlets, flyers, and web pages that give a brief overview. That's not really a surprise because most people learn about prayer by talking to other people. News of the examen spreads by word of mouth. But at some point a book might be helpful, at least for some people. I hope this is that book.

The examen isn't the only way to pray, but it's a way that everyone can pray. It banishes the abstract and relishes the concrete. It is inexhaustible. It treats every moment of every day as a blessed time when God can appear. It's a way to find God in all things.

2

why is this a good way to pray?

God is not remote from us. He is at the point
of my pen, my pick, my paint-brush, my
needle—and my heart and my thoughts.
—Pierre Theilhard de Chardin, SJ, *Hymn of the Universe*

What's not to like about the examen? It's simple; it's about the stuff we do every day; it connects us to God; it helps us walk with Christ in our daily rounds. It sounds like the perfect prayer. What's the catch?

I began to talk up the examen as soon as I started using it as a prayer practice, and it wasn't long before one of my friends gave me a skeptical look. "Why is sifting through our memories of the past twenty-four hours a sound way to pray?" she asked. Our memories aren't reliable. She told me a story about discovering that something she remembered very vividly never happened at all. She pointed out that we all filter our memories through preconceptions and desires; we tend to "remember" things the way we wish they had happened. Oh, and there was one other thing. The examen struck her as being very self-centered. She asked, "What's to keep it from becoming a play starring myself as the hero of a one-person show?"

Good questions. The examen doesn't make immediate sense to everyone; it isn't like most prayer. The examen is not liturgical prayer, devotional prayer, intercession, or prayer with scripture. It's not contemplation or centering prayer, which involve emptying our minds of images, words, and ideas. It's not the kind of prayer that lifts our hearts to a God who stands apart from our lives. From the perspective of capital "P" prayer, the examen hardly looks like prayer at all. It's a way of looking at ordinary life in a certain way. So why exactly is this a good way to pray?

The big theological answer

The theological answer is that God really is present in our world. He is *here*, not *up there*. Christianity has much in common with other religions, one of them being the practice of a discipline of self-scrutiny. But there are differences too, and the main one is the Christian belief that God became human in Jesus Christ. God's project of saving our world involves God becoming personally caught up in the lives his creatures lead. This is the doctrine of the Incarnation—the conviction that the God who created men and women has intimate knowledge of their lives because he is human as well as divine.

Personal is the key word. God is a community of three persons—Father, Son, and Holy Spirit—and the relationship we have with God is a personal one as well. The word for it is friendship, says Jesuit spiritual director William Barry. Nothing in our lives is so insignificant that it doesn't deserve God's attention. In fact, the mundane and the humdrum parts of our lives give depth and texture to our relationship with God. Washing the windows and cooking dinner are as much a part of the relationship as graduation day. If it's part of our human experience, God is in it.

> Nothing in our lives is so insignificant that it doesn't deserve God's attention.

God is present to us in many other ways too—in creation itself, in the scriptures, and in the history of the Christian community. We connect with God through many forms of prayer, including communal worship, silent meditation, devotional practices, and formal prayers. The examen focuses on God as present in our human experience. This doesn't represent our whole relationship with God but it's a vital part of it.

The down-to-earth practical answer

That's the theological argument for the examen. The other argument is a practical one. Experience shows that the examen can be a central element in a vibrant spiritual life.

The man who discovered this was St. Ignatius of Loyola. Ignatian spirituality, the spiritual tradition associated with Ignatius, has become a sophisticated discipline. There's a lot to it. People study it, write books about it, and earn doctorates in it. But Ignatian spirituality is also intensely practical. Just about everything to do with Ignatian spirituality originated in the life of Ignatius. Discernment, imaginative prayer, an approach to making decisions, and the other components of what later became Ignatian spirituality all sprang from Ignatius's needs and the needs of his friends. These spiritual practices were practical responses to real-world problems. Ignatius did not invent a spiritual system; he discovered certain truths, which he knew were true because he saw how they helped people thrive spiritually.

Ignatius was a careful and perceptive observer—a great "noticer." I imagine him as something of a detective in the spiritual realm. He noticed clues that eluded others. That's how he found God, and that's how the examen came about.

A soldier's daydreams

Ignatius was a Basque, coming from an ancient people in the mountains of northern Spain who had a reputation for toughness and independence. The young Ignatius was no saint; he was a soldier and a strutting courtier who liked the ladies. In 1515 he was arrested for street fighting, making him one of the few saints with a police record. In 1521, when he was about thirty, he was badly wounded in battle and spent many months recovering in his family castle. He became intolerably bored and asked for something to read. His literary tastes favored romances and adventure stories—the sixteenth-century equivalent of Harry Potter and John Grisham novels. He was disappointed to learn that the only books in the house were a life of Christ and a collection of stories about saints. Reluctantly, he read what was available.

Ignatius liked the religious books more than he thought he would. The life of Christ stirred him, and he was inspired by the lives of the saints. He imagined what it would be like doing heroic deeds for God as St. Francis and St. Dominic did (he surmised that he would do *better* than Francis and Dominic). After a while the lure of the saints diminished, and he took to daydreaming about his past life—his lady loves, the excitement of battle, and the deeds of derring-do that he hoped to accomplish again someday. Eventually these fantasies would recede, and he would again dream about the lives of the saints and imagined how good it would be to serve God. This is how Ignatius spent the lonely weeks and months of convalescence—alternating in his imagination between dreams of glory and romance and dreams of following Jesus.

The big question that loomed in the background was the one familiar to thirty-year-olds everywhere: what am I going to do with my life? Ignatius's dreams of military glory and knightly valor were just that—dreams.

His emotions were unsettled. Some days he would feel happy and confident; other days he would be restless and troubled. He began to notice a pattern in his feelings. Eventually the light bulb went on: his feelings were related to his imaginative life. His daydreams were always fun, but the emotions that followed them were different. He was joyful and confident after dreaming about following Christ. He was agitated and sad after daydreaming of machismo, lust, and honor.

Ignatius realized that these feelings weren't just fleeting moods; they had spiritual meaning. God was *in* the feelings of joy he felt after thinking about a life of service to God. Some other spirit, an "evil" spirit, was in the feelings of gloom and agitation that followed thoughts of his old life. He realized that something important was going on, that God was communicating with him through his emotions. The peace and joy seemed to point to the answer to the "what's next?" question. Before long Ignatius understood that the lasting fulfillment he sought would come by following Christ. For the rest of his life, Ignatius built on the insight he had received during those long months of recovery—that he could hear God by carefully attending to the movements of his inner life.

God in our experience

This is the "genesis story" of Ignatian spirituality because so many of its principles are seen here in embryonic form. One is that we can trust our experience. God spoke to Ignatius about the most important decision of his life through the emotions associated with his convalescence. Books and ideas and the counsel of the wise are fine, but the vital place where we find God is in what we ourselves experience. Like Ignatius, we can discern the right path by thoughtful reflection on our relationships with others, on our work in the world, and on the feelings generated by those encounters. The examen is a way to do this.

We can trust our experience because God deals with us directly. That's another principle of Ignatian spirituality. The church and scripture teach truth, and sacraments and devotional prayer nourish us, but God also communicates directly with each of us. We can have a personal relationship with God.

Another principle found at the beginning of Ignatius's story is the importance of the journey. Ignatius arose from his sickbed determined to serve God. But, especially during the early years after his conversion, he walked a meandering spiritual path full of U-turns, blind alleys, dead ends, false starts, and odd tangents. God was with Ignatius every step of the way. At the end of his life, Ignatius wrote a short autobiography in which he referred to himself in the third person as "the pilgrim." He saw his life as a journey, marked by deepening understanding of who God was and how he could best serve him.

My skeptical friend raised real issues; memories can be unreliable, and a prayer like the examen, in which we reflect on our experience, can become self-centered. But these are pitfalls to be avoided, not big red signs saying ROAD CLOSED. Ignatius found a way down the road. He developed the examen to help him to find God on the journey. We pray it for the same reason.

3

some problems that the examen solves (at least partly)

A quarter of an hour of attention is better
than a great many good works. Every time
that we really concentrate our attention,
we destroy the evil in ourselves.
—Simone Weil, *Waiting for God*

I've prayed in many different ways over the years. I had a solid cradle-Catholic upbringing, catching the tail end of the era of the Latin Mass, Saturday Confession, and home rosaries in my formative years. The Eucharist is central to my spiritual life. I love good liturgies. I liked the spontaneity of charismatic prayer in the 70s and 80s. I've tried to establish a habit of regular prayer, with mixed success. On top of that, I've been a magazine and book editor in Catholic publishing for many years. I've read a lot about prayer and written about it. Personally and professionally, I know about the Liturgy of the Hours, *lectio divina*, meditation, centering prayer, and contemplative prayer.

One of the things I know best about prayer is that it's often hard. Well-known difficulties arise; everybody who prays knows about them. I can't say that the examen has solved all my struggles with prayer; that's impossible and not even desirable. But the examen addresses some of my problems. I think that's the main reason for the examen's popularity. Millions of people pray it in pretty much the same way Ignatius prayed it in the sixteenth century because it's a practical approach to the difficulties most of us have with prayer. Here are some of them.

Where is God?

Prayer is contact with God, but where is God? Sometimes we feel God's closeness, but often we don't. This has been my experience and that of everybody I know who seriously tries to establish a habit of regular prayer. Many times I feel as if God has gone away on a long vacation and left me sitting in my quiet prayer place listening to the message he left on his answering machine. Spiritual teachers I admire say that God wants a personal relationship with me, that he wants to be *friends* with me, but frankly, that's hard to believe much of the time. Or rather, I believe it, but I don't experience it. Instead, the critical voice in my head asks, *Why should God care about my puny troubles?*

> Prayer is contact with God, but where is God?

Down this road lies the notion that God is master in the high distant heavens and that we're pretty much on our own down here. It's a functional deism—the religion of the rationalist Enlightenment philosophers who imagined God as a cosmic clockmaker who made the intricate mechanism of creation, wound it up, and left it to run on its own. We know this idea of God isn't true, but we sometimes act *as if* it were true.

In fact, the idea that God isn't around very much has a long pedigree in Christian history. I call it the "valley of tears" tradition, from a phrase in an old Catholic prayer. This tradition sees God as essentially absent from the world. Salvation comes at the end of this life, when we are delivered from our sorrowful journey through the valley of tears. Certainly we feel this way often enough. I suspect that Jesus' disciples might have felt this way in the aftermath of his ascension.

Another tradition emphasizes the incarnation—God entering into the world and humanity through the coming of Christ. God is *here* once and for all. The challenge is to find God in the midst of our human lives, which do in fact involve suffering, loss, and doubt. This is the precise problem that the examen is designed to solve. The whole prayer is an exercise in finding God. It assumes that God is present in our daily lives, and that his presence can be detected. If you think God is far away, pray the examen.

What do I pray about?

Before I started praying the examen regularly, the content of my prayer was a perpetual problem. I got tired of praying about the same things over and over—my family, my troubles, my friends' predicaments, my hope for the future. If I was tired of these things, surely God was too. I'd put aside intercessions and try to meditate, but I'd draw a big mental blank. A friend of mine summed it up when he described his prayer as "drifting in a pious coma."

> The examen is an immediate solution to the problem of "what do I pray about?"

The examen is an immediate solution to the problem of *what do I pray about*? The answer is: everything that's happened to you today. You might have the impression that your everyday life is the dreary same old, same old. It isn't. Daily life is rich and meaningful. Every encounter, every challenge, every disappointment, and every delight is a place where God can be found.

The Ben Franklin temptation

I slip easily into a self-centered do-it-yourself attitude—a kind of Ben Franklin-like, self-help mentality. A problem arises; I can solve it. An unforeseen muddle develops; I can fix it. My plans are thwarted? I can figure it out—on my own. (And I *hate* to ask for directions.) This attitude makes life difficult in many ways. It's positively toxic when applied to spiritual matters. It turns the spiritual life into a program of self-improvement.

The ancient Christians had a name for do-it-yourself spirituality: Pelagianism—a word derived from the name of a fourth-century heretic who taught that salvation comes through human effort, at least in part, and not solely from God. Pelagius had quite a following in his day, and his ideas are as popular today as they ever were. The idea that we can run our lives successfully by ourselves is so common in Western culture that we might as well call it our default mode.

The examen makes it hard to be a smug Pelagian. One aspect of the examen that is particularly useful in combating the Ben Franklin temptation is the attitude of thanksgiving and gratitude that permeates the whole exercise. We pray the examen in the realization that God has given us everything. He showers us with his gifts—the gift of life, of family and friends, of fruitful work. Even the ability to thank and praise God is one of God's gifts. By reminding us that we are not God, the examen shatters the illusion that the world revolves around me.

Woe is me

The sunny, all-is-well, Ben Franklin optimism has an evil twin: gloomy negativity. The valley-of-tears tradition encourages a grim outlook that sees life as dominated by a furious struggle with sin. For many people, prayer has become little more than a depressing catalog of sins, lapses, and errors.

> The whole point of the examen is to make a balanced, accurate appraisal of our experience.

Of course failure and regret are part of life, and any accurate appraisal of our experience will involve looking at them. But our prayer shouldn't be gloomy. The examen helps by directing our attention away from ourselves. "Woe is me" prayer is basically self-centered. But examen prayer is God-centered. The context for looking at our troubles and failings is gratitude to God for the blessings of our lives. The whole point of the examen is to make a balanced, accurate appraisal of our experience. Our sins will surface, but in the context of a relationship with a loving God who has given us the great gift of life.

Let's pretend

The most insidious problem in prayer is the game of "let's pretend." This is the urge to put on a good face when we pray. It's the desire to be a different person—someone who is kinder, more generous, more loving, holier than the person you really are. Sitting down to pray feels like a job interview with an amiable but enigmatic boss. You look your best, you put out positive vibes. You project an appealing version of yourself. It's not entirely false, but it's not entirely accurate either. To say that this gives prayer an air of artificiality is an understatement. "Let's pretend" is also hard work.

For years I had a terrible time praying because I thought that prayer was for good people. I prayed when I felt virtuous; I avoided it when I felt guilty or ashamed or defeated, which meant that I didn't pray much for long stretches. I eventually realized that it was OK to be honest with God.

There's a scene in the movie *The Apostle* that dramatizes honest prayer. Sonny Dewey, a Pentecostal minister played by Robert Duvall, has lost his wife and his church. He goes up in the attic of his mother's house and rages at God. "I'm confused, I'm mad, I love you, Lord, I love you but I am mad at you!" he roars. When a neighbor calls the house to complain about the noise, his mother explains, "Sometimes Sonny talks to the Lord and sometimes he yells at the Lord. Tonight he happens to be yelling at him."

The examen is an excellent way to be honest in prayer. We review our day in the loving light of Christ precisely to strip away facades and correct self-delusions. It helps us say, "Here I am, Lord, warts and all." A Jesuit I admire calls prayer "a long loving look at the real." The examen is a way to see the real. "No illusions" is a good motto for the examen.

Get acquainted with your feelings

Suppressing feelings is a big part of let's-pretend prayer. You don't want strong emotions to leak out during the job interview. But examen prayer takes feelings very seriously. This is one of its great attractions.

This idea made me nervous when I was learning about the examen. I thought that my feelings were at best irrelevant. Why would God be interested in the irritation I felt sitting in a traffic jam or my anxiety about the fate of a project I was working on? At worst, feelings seemed dangerous. How could paying attention to my shifting moods be anything but a distraction from the real business of connecting with God?

It's true that feelings aren't the supreme arbiter of authentic experience—prayer is not a branch of therapy. But feelings are a large part of our day-to-day lives, and if God reveals himself in our conscious experience, he will be found in the feelings we have as we go about our day. Fear, delight, boredom, peace, disgust— these and other feelings are signposts, warning flares, and waving flags. They say: look over here. Something important is going on.

Recall the insight that Ignatius had while he was recovering. He realized that his *feelings*, not his thoughts, pointed in the right direction. When he imagined a life of following Christ, he felt excitement and joy. When he imagined a life of military adventure, he felt listless and depressed. This started him on the road to conversion.

One way to pray the examen is to focus on one feeling you've had recently and ask God to show you what it means. It might be a strong feeling that lingers in your awareness, or something subtle and fleeting that the Holy Spirit brings to mind as you pray. It might be a positive feeling—elation, satisfaction, peace. Or it might be something troubling—anger, depression, worry. Ask God to reveal what's behind this emotion. Where does it come from? What does it tell you about yourself and the way you live your life? What might God want you to do about it?

> One way to pray the examen is to focus on one feeling you've had recently and ask God to show you what it means.

Don't worry that this kind of prayer is an invitation to let emotions take over your life. Allowing feelings to surface in the context of gratitude and prayerful openness to God is a good way to address them without becoming overwhelmed. By asking God what they mean, we make them vehicles of grace instead of unruly passions that take us down.

Solving "the Christian problem"

One day I was riding a subway in New York City and engaging in my favorite New York pastime: people watching. You can really study people on the subway because they sit in the same place for a while and they almost always avoid eye contact. Across from me sat a Sikh man wearing an expensive suit and a turban. Near him was a Muslim woman also wearing a head covering. Down the car a bit were two Hasidic Jews wearing long black coats and flat-brimmed black hats, and sporting curls of hair on the sides of their heads. The religions of the world, all in one subway car—only in New York. Then I noticed that the man sitting next to the Sikh appeared to be reading a Bible. It was hard to tell for sure. The book looked ordinary enough, but the type was small and laid out in two columns on the page. The guy looked like everyone else, an ordinary guy reading a book on a subway. The other believers were easy to spot because they were dressed in a way that announced their faith to the world. The Christian guy (if he was a Christian) blended in pretty well. So did I.

A friend of mine, writer Chris Lowney, calls this "the Christian problem." The problem is: how are Christians different? Our lives look pretty much the same as everyone's. Some Christians live in monasteries and a fortunate few are free enough to go to daily Mass and pray frequently through the day. The rest of us bob along on a river of emails, meetings, housework, errands, commuting, and to-do lists—just as everyone does. We watch the same TV shows and go to the same movies. "They'll know we are Christians by our love," says the refrain of an old song, but non-Christians also try to behave ethically and treat others well. In everyday terms, what makes us different?

Other religions have answers to that question, as my subway inspection showed. Observant Jews follow halakhah, the Jewish Law, which regulates food, dress, and other aspects of daily life. Faithful Muslims pray five times a day. Hindus are differentiated into caste groups with distinct modes of dress and behavior. We Christians have few of these outer signs of religious identity.

That's because Jesus wasn't really interested in external signs of piety. He was much more interested in the condition of our hearts. We act as Christians when our hearts are set on loving God and other people. We live as followers of Christ when we're aligned with the work God is doing in the world. This is much more a matter of our inner orientation than outward characteristics. We know we are Christians when we are attuned to God's presence "at the point of my pen, my pick, my paint-brush, my needle—and my heart and my thoughts," as Pierre Theilhard de Chardin wrote.

The answer to the Christian problem is to find God in all things, to see God in what we think, do, and feel—in life with family, friends, colleagues, and casual acquaintances, in our busyness and our rest. That's what the examen helps us do. That's why I call it the prayer that changes everything.

step one:
pray for light

What does it matter? Grace is everywhere.
—Georges Bernanos, *The Diary of a Country Priest*

I don't pray the examen in precisely the same way Ignatius did. I begin it differently. There's a reason for that.

Ignatius lays out the examen in five brief points in section 43 of the *Spiritual Exercises*. (I'll identify quotations from the *Exercises* by section number.) The first of these is to give thanks ("Give thanks to God our Lord for favors received," he writes). The second is to pray for enlightenment from God ("Ask for grace to know my sins and to rid myself of them."). I reverse these steps. I begin the examen by asking God for the light and grace to do what I can't do on my own.

I do this because I need a constant reminder that I am not God. I'm afflicted by the illusion that I know what's best for me and for everyone else who crosses my path. Show me a problem; I can solve it. Are you uncertain, troubled, perplexed? I can clear things up for you. My profession reinforces this illusion of mastery. I am an editor—a professional critic. I've spent my career spotting the flaws in articles and book manuscripts and telling writers how to fix them. Even better, I fix them myself, and I'm pretty good at this. It feeds the illusion that I know best.

But I don't know best. I don't know what's best for myself, and I certainly don't know what's best for anyone else. It's taken me a long time to grasp the fact that I'm not God. I need the grace of God to do anything worthwhile. I can't even get up in the morning and face the day without him.

The experience of praying the examen helped me realize this. When I first began praying it, I began by giving thanks, just as Ignatius says. But this didn't always go well. Many days I didn't *feel* like giving thanks. Many days I didn't *feel* like praying the examen at all. It seemed like a better idea to forget about my lousy day and read a book or watch television or check my email. I would make myself give thanks, but this seemed like an exercise in willpower—something I do under my own power.

So I decided to begin praying the examen by asking God to give me the grace to pray. This is surrender. I'm giving up the struggle to run my life and asking the Holy Spirit to take control. Everything in my life—including the ability to give thanks—comes as a gift from God. Since I made this adjustment, praying the examen has been easier. I like the constant reminder that I need God to do what I want to do.

I think that rearranging the order of the examen would be OK with Ignatius. Ignatius was always flexible in his advice and methods. "The Spiritual Exercises must be adapted to the condition of the one who engages in them," he wrote (18), and this surely applies to the examen as well. As you gain experience with praying the examen, don't hesitate to adapt it. "Whatever works" is an Ignatian motto.

What kind of light are we praying for?

We pray for a specific grace at the beginning of the examen. We want to see our everyday life through God's eyes. Jesus promised us that "the Spirit of truth . . . will guide you to all truth" (John 16:13). This isn't some vague spiritual promise. The Holy Spirit is a real force operating in our lives. We invoke the Holy Spirit at the beginning of the examen prayer to show us what we cannot see ourselves. As St. Paul wrote, we want "the Spirit that is from God, so that we may understand the gifts bestowed on us by God" (1 Corinthians 2:11).

We're acknowledging that God's perspective is *different* from our own. We're looking for spirit-guided insight, not an examen that relies solely on the powers of our natural memory. But we're not looking for miraculous supernatural intervention either. There are no voices from on high in the Ignatian examen. I haven't heard any voices myself, and spiritual directors that I admire say that such experiences are quite rare. God ordinarily works through natural processes. With the examen, the process we use is the human faculty of memory. As my friend noted, memory is fallible, unpredictable, and sometimes muddled, but we approach the daily examen with the conviction that the Holy Spirit will use our imperfect abilities for trustworthy insights. Why should it be any different? This blend of the human and the divine is the central reality of the Christian mystery. God acts through human means. What we experience in the examen is precisely the great mystery that God is present in our experience of everyday life in our workaday world.

> What we experience in the examen is precisely the great mystery that God is present in our experience of everyday life in our workaday world.

George Aschenbrenner, SJ, put it well in a famous essay about the examen: "We begin the examen with an explicit petition for that enlightenment which will occur in and through our own powers but which our own natural powers could never be capable of all by themselves."

There are no burning bushes or booming voices from Mount Sinai in the examen. God appears in the quiet whisper of our Spirit-guided memories, thoughts, and feelings. What an awesome reality!

Why do we want light?

This is what Ignatius said we're to do in this phase of the examen: "Ask for grace to know my sins and to rid myself of them." This is a prayer of petition; we're asking for something. Actually, we're asking for three things: 1) grace; 2) to know; 3) to be free.

"Grace" means "gift." We pray that God will give us the gift to see through God's eyes. Another way to put it is that we are petitioning God to give us the gift of seeing God's gifts to us.

We pray "to know." What do we want to know? Whatever God cares to show us, of course, but certain matters are bound to come up again and again, and it's a good idea to pray specifically to know about them.

The most important of these is relationships. I'm hard-pressed to think of anything that goes on in my life that *doesn't* involve relationships. One day in the examen I was wrestling with the big question "Who am I, really?" and I decided to make a list of my various identities. I'm a husband (wife: Susan); father (Dave, Sarah, Laura, Carolyn); brother (Joe and John); nephew (Jean, Jerry, Joe, and John); uncle (twelve nieces and nephews); father-in-law (John, Drew, Jennifer); grandfather (Signe, Brett, Kirsten); cousin (about fifty first cousins, no kidding); friend (lots of names there); colleague (bunch of people); employee (Loyola Press); parishioner (St. Mary Student Parish, Ann Arbor); volunteer (Down Syndrome Support Team of Southeastern Michigan); blogger (dotMagis); neighbor (the people on Lois Court). What else? I'm a customer of numerous business establishments, a citizen who tries to be well-informed, and a baseball fan. That's me, pretty much. Everything is a relationship. (I'll admit that my relationship with the Detroit Tigers is one-sided, but it involves a lot of emotion.)

You might want to make your own list. You'll find, as I did, that most of your life involves your connections with other people. That's where you find your joy and your pain. That's what you'll be reviewing in the daily examen. It's a good idea to ask God to show you what you need to know about these relationships. Ask to know what's *really* going on here. Our common tendency is to consider relationships from a self-centered point of view. We ask, "How am *I* doing?" In the examen we want to know, "How are *they* doing?" We want to look at the whole relationship, not just our part in it.

Joseph Tetlow, SJ, a celebrated spiritual director, says that we look at our relationships to make sure that we are loving the way Jesus loves. Ignatius said this about love: "Love ought to manifest itself in deeds rather than in words," and that love consists in mutual sharing (230-1). In other words, we love by *doing* things and by sharing what we have.

Here's a prayer that Fr. Tetlow wrote, asking God for light about relationships. You might find it helpful.

> *Spirit of the risen Lord,*
> *who moved the Holy One to care for friends*
> *with his still wounded hands and pierced heart –*
> *make me attentive to my friends*
> *even with my fearing touch and wearing spirit.*
> *Open my eyes to see what gifts they really are;*
> *open my ears to hear what good*
> *they really mean to say.*
> *Brace my spirit to feel what they need me to feel.*
> *And as you steeled the heart of Jesus*
> *while he lived misunderstood and they betrayed,*
> *brace me now while I find how I have fared*
> *in risking my self to remain true to who I am*
> *and to be open in giving and receiving love.*
> *Amen.*

What do I really want?

We pray for grace. We pray to know. The third thing we pray for is to be free—"to rid myself" of my sins. Sin in the Ignatian perspective includes the whole panoply of ideas, dreams, desires, longings, and hungers that keep us from becoming the kind of people we were meant to be. Ignatius called them "disordered attachments." They are desires that are literally "disordered"—out of order, out of whack. A reasonable desire to make money becomes raging greed. A yearning for love becomes riotous lust. Disordered attachments are priorities gone wrong.

Ignatius's program for spiritual maturity is an effort to rid oneself of these disordered attachments. Once free, we can answer a single question: What do I really want? That is, when you shed your fears and resentments, when you disentangle yourself from other people's ideas of what constitutes "the good life," when you get free of bogus promises and spurious dreams, what do you *really* want? Ignatius believed that when we know the answer to that question, we will know what God wants too.

That's a remarkably optimistic view of the human personality. It's not Freudian—Ignatius knew nothing of libidos and ids and Oedipus complexes, and he would have rejected the claim that they drive our behavior. The Ignatian view is not Calvinist— Ignatius didn't think that the human soul was so irreparably damaged by sin that it is incapable of knowing the good. The Ignatian view does not completely match the religious education of my youth, which viewed desires with grave suspicion. Ignatius loved desires. In the *Spiritual Exercises*, he continually tells us to pray for what we want. He believed that our deepest desires—what he called the "great desires"—are for loving union with God and others. These are the deepest truths about ourselves and the fundamental forces that drive us.

This puts a different spin on "sin." Yes, we sin because we're willful and full of pride, but we sin mainly because we're ignorant. We don't know what we really want, so we pursue fantasies, pale reflections of that which will fulfill us. We sin not because we have desires, but because we are ignorant of the "desires beneath the desires." We sin not because we are in touch with our desires, but because we are *not* in touch with them.

What do I really want? That's the Big Idea that ties all this together. This is the question we most want to answer and the reason we pray the examen. This big idea inspires us to be a better spouse, friend, neighbor, and worker.

What do I really want? is the question lurking in the background of our prayer at the beginning of the examen. When we answer this question, we are on our way to freedom. Only God can show us this, and God's light is what we ask for at the beginning of the examen prayer.

step two: give thanks

'Twas my last gratitude
When I slept— at night—
'Twas the first Miracle
Let in—with Light—
—Emily Dickenson

A friend of mine wanted to talk, so we went out for coffee. He had many troubles: his business, a small ad agency, was struggling. His ex-wife was sick and wanted to borrow money from him. He didn't care for his daughter's new boyfriend. An old back problem had flared up. He winced in pain as he sat in the café, telling me how worried and fearful he felt.

I listened, sympathized, and eventually suggested that he think about the things he could be grateful for. There were many; I mentioned some of them. My friend listened, thanked me, and said he'd try to do that. But he also looked at me sadly and said, "Being grateful doesn't feel real. It feels like putting on a pair of rose-colored glasses."

I sympathized with that feeling too. I've had some spells of depression. I know what it feels like to be mired in melancholy and have loved ones urging me to "think about things differently" and therapists showing me ways to "reframe the problem." It sounds like a trick, and I can understand why my friend thought that my exhortations to be grateful came across as a deliberate effort to *not* see things as they really are.

Adopting "an attitude of gratitude" can be a practical stratagem to get through a tough time. But the kind of gratitude that Ignatius was talking about when he tells us to "give thanks to God our Lord for the favors received" is something deeper and stronger. It's the heart of prayer. Such gratitude is a window into the deepest truth about ourselves—that we are caught up in a relationship with a loving God who is generous beyond our imagining. When we catch sight of this, giving thanks is the right response. Gratitude isn't a pair of rose-colored glasses; it's the essence of our spiritual condition.

A God who gives

Gratitude is the hallmark of Ignatian spirituality. I've known several people who epitomize the spirit of the Ignatian way. Their distinguishing characteristic is a spirit of gratitude for all things. One of them likes to quote a line from Shakespeare's play *Twelfth Night*: "I can no other answer make but thanks, and thanks, and ever thanks." Gratitude is the key to Ignatian spirituality in two senses—the key that unlocks the door, and the key in which the music is played. It's both the context of prayer and the secret that explains everything.

Ignatius was hardly the first Christian to understand the importance of gratitude. "In all circumstances give thanks," Paul writes in First Thessalonians, probably the oldest text in the New Testament. But Ignatius emphasized gratitude to a remarkable degree. Once he established a connection to God, he immediately began to perceive God as a generous giver of gifts. He saw himself as a student; God was the teacher, filling him with insight and understanding. St. Francis was in love with Christ the poor man. St. Benedict loved community and hospitality. St. Ignatius was caught up in a vision of God the giver of an endless stream of gifts.

> Gratitude is the hallmark of Ignatian spirituality.

This vision is expressed in a striking way at the end of the *Spiritual Exercises* in a meditation that Ignatius called the Contemplation to Attain the Love of God. The Spiritual Exercises is a long retreat. This meditation draws the retreat to a close; it is the image of God that we're to carry out into daily life and our work in the world.

We're to ponder "how much God our Lord has done for me, and how much he has given me of what he possesses." We're to imagine "all blessings and gifts as descending from above . . . as the rays of light descend from the sun, and as the waters flow from their fountain." We meditate on how God "dwells in me and gives me being, life, sensation, intelligence." We think about "how God works and labors for me in all creatures upon the face of the earth" (234-237). This is God—endlessly bestowing gifts like rays from the sun, ceaselessly working, infinitely generous.

Ignatius prefaces the contemplation with two remarks about love. He says that love is manifested "in deeds rather than in words," and that it "consists in a mutual sharing of goods" (230–31). How does God love us? He *shares* himself and actively *does* concrete deeds. How do we love God? By doing the same. We share ourselves with God. Our response is Ignatius's most famous prayer:

> Take, Lord, receive all my liberty, my memory, my understanding, and my entire will. All I have and call my own. Whatever I have or hold, you have given me. I restore it all to you and surrender it wholly to be governed by your will. Give me only your love and grace and I am rich enough and ask for nothing more. (234)

We give God what he doesn't have—our freedom, memory, understanding, and will. We do this out of gratitude, for graces received.

The worst thing in the world

It's impossible to exaggerate how important gratitude is to Ignatius's worldview; it's absolutely central. It's so important that he considered *ingratitude* to be the deadliest sin. Out of all sins and evils, he wrote, "ingratitude is one of the things most worthy of detestation." So much so, he continued, that ingratitude is "the cause, beginning, and origin of all evils and sins." If someone asked you to name the origin of all evils, how high would ingratitude rank on your list? Not very high, I'll bet. I would probably choose the old standby, pride, or one of the other seven deadly sins such as greed, anger, or envy. The idea that ingratitude is a lethal wrong probably wouldn't occur to me.

One reason is that the word "gratitude" doesn't have the same clout in our culture that it did in Ignatius's time. For us, ingratitude is akin to having bad manners. When we were raising our children, my wife and I taught them to thank people for gifts and to say "thank you" when adults complimented them or gave hospitality. Sometimes I notice when people don't say thank you when I think they should, but this is more of a mild irritation than a grave offense. (I think that my annoyed reaction is worse than the perceived ingratitude.) In Ignatius's late-medieval society, gratitude was taken much more seriously. It was a highly esteemed virtue. Society was organized around a set of mutual obligations. Understanding and acknowledging services rendered was part of the glue that bound people together.

Cultural differences are only part of the story, however. In his emphasis on gratitude, Ignatius was on to something vitally important. Gratitude is a fundamental part of our relationship with God. Ingratitude is something like willful blindness to the truth.

To be truly grateful, we need to think about God in a certain way. In a letter to a friend, Ignatius remarked, "We will sooner tire of receiving his gifts than he of giving them." This is a picture of God that's very different from some common ones: the scorekeeper God who keeps track of our sins; the transcendent, remote God who presides over creation from a throne in eternity; the demanding God who's after us to do more, better, faster. Instead, we are in a relationship with a God who is the infinitely generous giver of gifts. It's an unequal relationship to be sure, but it's a real relationship nonetheless. Gratitude is its lifeblood.

Practicing gratitude

Don't rush through this step. Gratitude isn't a preliminary to the real meat of the examen. It's actually the other way around: the examen instills gratitude. Take as much time with this step as seems right. I try to allow the Holy Spirit to guide me here. You might focus your entire examen on this step for a time, particularly if you are just beginning to pray this way. Take this sentence from the *Spiritual Exercises* and slowly do what it says: "I will ponder with great affection how much God our Lord has done for me, and how much He has given Me of what He possesses, and finally, how much . . . the same Lord desires to give Himself to me" (234).

Humility helps too. God is showering me with gifts—a pleasant thought, blessed am I. But if all is gift, we don't own anything ourselves. Without God we have nothing. George Aschenbrenner, SJ, puts it this way: "The stance of a Christian in the midst of the world is that of a poor person, possessing nothing, not even himself, and yet being gifted at every instance and through everything." This thought—I'm a poor man who's constantly receiving gifts—helps me give thanks.

Human beings seem to have a built-in urge to pray. But for many of us, gratitude doesn't come naturally. Speaking for myself, I'm much more inclined to take note of what I *don't* have than to thank anybody for what I *do* have. I take my blessings for granted.

We begin the examen with prayers of gratitude, but it's also true that the examen will develop within us the habit of gratitude. It does this by focusing our attention on specific, tangible gifts that God has given us.

Virtues and spiritual blessings can become vague and abstract. The examen's process of reflective thanksgiving makes them concrete. In time, gratitude can become an element of our everyday attitude. Now that's something to be grateful for.

6

step three:
review the day

God works with what is.
—Bernie Owens, SJ

My friend Pete, a family practice physician, tells me about a typical day:

> I walk into the office at 8:30 and it starts right up. Lab reports to look at. Questions from the nurses. Patient appointments every fifteen minutes. The phone rings all day. Patients need to talk to me. Other doctors need to talk to me and I need to talk to them. Problems appear. Go, go, go. Some days my schedule blows up completely. I have a long list of important but not urgent things that I never seem to get to. It's madness.

But it's not really madness. It's Pete's life, and Pete doesn't think his life is meaningless or intolerably chaotic. The tool that helps him stay grounded is the examen, which he prays every morning (he's too tired to pray at night). He's usually able to find a meaningful connection with God when he reviews his day.

"It's funny," Pete says. "I get into trouble when I *think* too much about what I do—like, thinking about what it all *means*. When I think about my life in general, I get worried. When I just look at my life as it is, I'm in much better shape spiritually."

Be real. Stay in the moment. I'm sure you've heard these slogans before. I've heard this advice for mental and spiritual health so often that I don't really listen to it anymore. I nod my head yes and go on to the next thing. Chances are you do too. So let's stay here a moment.

Being real

In the examen, we're talking about being real in two senses. The first is the concrete reality of everyday life; this is the subject of the examen. The second sense is the reality beneath the reality. We're looking to strip away our disordered attachments and get at what we really want.

The importance of reality in the first sense was impressed upon me by a Jesuit named Bernie Owens. At a workshop he gave on discernment of spirits, a meandering discussion developed about which circumstances were conducive to discernment and which weren't. The discussion grew somewhat speculative—what if this happens, what if it's that. Fr. Owens stopped that talk and said, "Let's not forget: God works with what is." He went on, "God doesn't work with what was, or should have been, or what might be." I still have the legal pad with my notes from that session. In capital letters, are the words GOD WORKS WITH WHAT IS.

The examen is an exercise in finding God in your life as you are living it *right now*. The past is prologue and the future hasn't happened yet. You look at the present. You summon the memories of the hours you have just lived and try to experience those events as you lived them. Yes, you are aware that events and relationships in the past have shaped today's circumstances.

> God doesn't work with what was, or should have been, or what might be. **GOD WORKS WITH WHAT IS.**

Yes, you will eventually be making decisions that will shape your future. But at this moment in the daily examen you are looking at *what is*.

It's very easy to avoid dealing with what is, right now. My specialty is speculative revision of the past. I should have had a better explanation about why I was late to that meeting. I shouldn't have put off that task; now I might not finish it in time. My brother was grumpy when he came over to watch football; I should have cheered him up somehow. If only, if only . . . Many things *might* have happened. The examen looks at what *did* happen: I was late for a meeting. I didn't make a good decision about my work. Something seems to be lacking in my relationship with my brother.

Walter Burghardt, SJ, says this about the real. "The real I look at. I do not analyze or argue it, describe or define it; I am one with it. I do not move around it; I enter into it. Lounging by a stream, I do not exclaim 'Ah, H_2O!' I let the water trickle gently through my fingers. I do not theologize about the redemptive significance of Calvary; I link a pierced hand to mine."

But that's only part of the story. The examen is concerned with the real and the present, but it's not a Zen-like immersion into the wordless eternal now. We pray the examen to discern the deeper truth about ourselves. God is present in the examen as well as in the activities of our everyday lives. The examen is guided by the Holy Spirit. We expect to see our lives through God's eyes, not our own. We do the examen to discover: Where is God? How do I respond to him? What do I want most of all?

The language of feelings

Here's what Ignatius said about the third step of the examen: "The third point is to demand an account of my soul from the time of rising up to the present examination. I should go one hour after another, one period after another. The thoughts should be examined first, then the words, and finally, the deeds" (43). The first part seems clear enough; Ignatius recommends going through the day in sequential order. The last sentence isn't so clear. What did he mean by "the thoughts should be examined first, then the words, and finally, the deeds?"

Deeds, surprisingly, are last. This is the same Ignatius who said that love is manifested in deeds rather than words. But for this part of the examen, what we do is less important than the "thoughts" and the "words." What are these? George Aschenbrenner, SJ, says that "thoughts" and "words" are best understood as referring to our emotions. He says, "it is here in the depths of our affectivity, so spontaneous, strong, and shadowy at times, that God moves us and deals with us most intimately."

This is one of Ignatius's most important insights. Recall the story of his conversion, in which he discerned the right direction for his life by interpreting the shifts in his feelings as he contemplated options for the future. Ignatius made our emotional life part of prayer. He made it much easier to grasp the spiritual significance of our feelings by developing a vocabulary for the tumult that goes on in our inner lives.

Ignatius classified spiritual feelings and emotions into two broad categories. He called the first category *consolation*. This describes feelings that move us toward God and others. Consolation is any felt increase in faith, hope, and love. It is commonly experienced as feelings of peace, security, and joy. The second category is *desolation*. It's the opposite of consolation—anything that takes us away from the love of God and others. We experience desolation as a troubled spirit: anxiety, restlessness, doubts, self-loathing, and dejection. One of the surest signs of desolation is spiritual lethargy. If you think that God is nowhere to be found, and that it's not worth the trouble to establish contact, you're probably in a state of desolation. Other signs of desolation are feelings of self-pity and meaninglessness. If you feel incompetent and your work seems pointless, desolation has settled on your soul.

In praying the examen, we reflect on these various feelings. Consolation and desolation are not rarified spiritual states; they are feelings and moods that we experience all the time. We often push them out of our awareness as we go about the business of our day. In the examen we look at them carefully.

Where has God been in our day? We find him in those times when we have felt happy, joyous, and at peace. We also find him in times of anxiety and sadness, because we need God at those times.

What we *do* and how we *think* are of great consequence. But first we ask how we *feel*. There, "in the depths of our affectivity," we find the Holy Spirit powerfully moving us.

Ways to review the day

The examen is a tool, not a prescribed system, and like any tool it can be used in many ways. If you are led by the Holy Spirit when you pray the examen, you will find your own way to pray it, and you are likely to pray it differently as time goes on. You might flounder around for a while at first. That's OK. It's your examen and your life. Learn how to use this tool with your own unique style and flair.

Here are some ideas about how you might do the review of the day. I offer them in the spirit of freedom and flexibility that Ignatius valued so much.

The first idea comes from Ignatius himself: go through the day in sequence—"one hour after another, one period after another."

Begin with how you felt when you woke up. Think about the dreams you had during the night, if you can remember them. Go through the events of the day one hour after another—the places you've been, the people you encountered, the work you did. Be attentive to the feelings that arise as you play this home movie in your memory. Strong feelings—positive and negative—are usually signals of where the action was in your day. Let them surface, look at them, ask the Holy Spirit to show you what they are saying about God's presence in your life and your response to it. Also be attentive to weaker, subtler feelings. Sometimes we're barely aware of intuitions that are quieter but also important.

An approach I particularly like is to take *one* of these feelings and pray from it. It might be the strongest feeling you remember—a moment of anger or an intense feeling of satisfaction. It might be the predominant feeling of the day—a restlessness, a calm serenity, a mild funk, or a serene peace. Or the feeling might be something small and fleeting, something you've forgotten that the Holy Spirit brings to mind. Use this as a springboard for prayerful reflection. What does this mean? Where does it fit in?

This suggestion comes from Dennis Hamm, SJ, in an article on the examen called "Rummaging for God." Fr. Hamm likens the examen to rummaging around in a drawer full of stuff—keys, lists, gadgets, odds and ends, and just plain junk. The drawer is everything that happened that day; you're searching for the couple of objects that especially speak of God's presence and love. The examen is the rummaging, and it's hard to tell in advance what's going to turn up.

One day during my examen, I remembered a moment of irritation I felt when some computer software I was using didn't work the way I expected. This seemed insignificant, but reflection brought out a lot more. I was also frustrated by the job I was using the software for, which wasn't going the way I wanted. And I was angry at someone I was working with. I was glad to learn all of this, and I prayed for the patience and humility that I needed more urgently than I thought.

Another suggestion is to review your day from a particular perspective. It's like filtering your email through certain categories, or querying a database for specific information.

Try reviewing your day through the filter of your particular gifts. The infinitely generous Giver of gifts has equipped you with certain talents—the things you do especially well. An old teacher of mine said that you know the work you are especially suited for when you can do it for a long time without getting tired. My cousin Jack is a physician who runs a clinic that primarily serves migrant workers and their families. He often works eighty- and ninety-hour weeks. I asked him once how he managed to do this. He said, "I'm good at it. I enjoy it. I honestly don't get tired." ("At least until I get home," he added.)

What have you done with your gifts lately? You are a good listener. Did you listen to anybody today? You have a talent for organizing. What have you done to bring order out of chaos lately? A woman I know is an artist. She wants to do something every day to use her talent, even if it's a very small thing, and she regularly reviews that commitment in her examen.

Another filter you can use to review your day is to evaluate the state of your relationships. I've found it surprisingly easy to take my relationships for granted. I often think about them when I pray the examen. Should something more be happening in this relationship? Does anything need repair? When you ask yourself these questions you might find yourself wondering, What is *really* going on this relationship? Why is there distance between me and this person? Why have I found such delight in getting together with this friend? The rhythm of the examen consists of questions like these: Why am I drawn to this? Why am I avoiding that? What's going on here? What do I *really* want?

In the review of the day, we are especially interested in our *response* to God. God is relentlessly, abundantly active. We've seen how Ignatius depicts God pouring out his gifts "like the light rays from the sun." Our challenge is to respond. Jesus calls; we answer. The dynamic is like the call and response of a gospel choir. He invites us to join him—the same way he invited fishermen, tax collectors, sinners, and idle bystanders in the Gospel stories. We respond—eagerly or grudgingly, wholeheartedly or fitfully. The examen is a way to keep track of the quality of our response.

"His life was good but his thinking was bad"

One of my favorite characters in fiction is Konstantin Dmitrich Levin, a central figure in Leo Tolstoy's great novel *Anna Karenina*. Levin is an intelligent, energetic young aristocrat with a powerful conscience and a strong thirst for truth. Like many of his educated and wealthy friends, he has abandoned the Orthodox Christianity of his childhood; but unlike them he seeks answers to the meaning of life. The death of his brother precipitates an existential crisis. Levin understands for the first time that nothing lies ahead for him (and everyone else) but "suffering, death, and eternal oblivion." He can't accept this; he must "either explain his life so that it did not look like the wicked mockery of some devil, or shoot himself."

He reads widely in philosophy and theology. He talks to learned men. He spends hours in tormented reflection. Nothing satisfies his yearning for meaning. His intellectual despair deepens so badly that he hides ropes and guns, fearing that he will take his own life.

One day a peasant says of a friend, "He's an upright old man. He lives for the soul. He remembers God." The words strike Levin powerfully and cause a rethinking. He perceives a vast difference between his thinking and his life. His thinking was a tormented search for ideas that might give meaning to his existence. Meanwhile he has fallen in love and married a woman who loves him very much. He actively manages a large estate. He's responsible for the well-being of his brother, sister, and an extended family. His son is born. He is busy with a wide circle of friends. He takes on civic responsibilities.

> God can be found when we look at life as we actually live it.

How ironic, Levin says. He thinks that life is meaningless, but the life that he actually lives is busy, productive, and satisfying. What did this mean? he asks. "It meant that his life was good, but his thinking was bad." His reasoning tells him that life is a pitiless struggle for survival that rewards selfishness and power. But he doesn't really believe that, and he certainly doesn't live that way. In his everyday life he lives for an ideal of the good.

His actions are guided by "the presence of an infallible judge who decided which of two possible actions was better and which was worse." Like the peasant's friend, "he lives for the soul. He remembers God."

Levin is just a character in a novel (though I'm told that he's a lot like Tolstoy). But I love his story because it shows how God can be found when we look at life as we actually live it. Levin shows how the examen can change everything.

step four:
face what's wrong

The problem is that I am from a
dysfunctional family, work in a
dysfunctional job, and am surrounded by
neurotics, with whom I fit perfectly.
—Joseph Tetlow, SJ

One winter afternoon I was changing planes in Chicago on my way to a family funeral in New York. A beloved uncle had died, and I was feeling sad, but that doesn't excuse what I did on Concourse A in Midway airport.

It was lunch time, and I bought a hamburger at a well-known fast-food vendor. It was crowded, so I took my meal a couple of dozen yards down the concourse to the eating area of another fast-food restaurant. It was nearly deserted. I stood at a high table near the concourse and began to eat my hamburger.

Then a man pushing a trash cart came by. He was very small and bent over, a janitor, a man who does more physical work in a day than I do in month. He looked at me and then pointed to a small sign over my head that I hadn't seen: THIS AREA FOR [THIS FAST-FOOD COMPANY'S] PATRONS ONLY. The little man pointed to my food bag stamped with the logo of another fast-food company, and said "Look at the sign. You can't eat here."

Instantly, I was enraged. "You're kidding." Then, "There's no one else here." Then, "Mind your own business." Finally, I held out my arms, hands together, palms down, and said, "Put the cuffs on. Take me in." The janitor shook his head sadly and pushed his cart away, looking as humiliated as I had hoped he would be for daring to interfere with someone as important as myself.

I was immediately ashamed of myself. I stewed over what I did for a couple of minutes and then started to look for the guy to apologize, but I couldn't find him and then my flight was called. I had a long flight to New York to think things over.

I'd like to say that the arrogant guy who suddenly flared up in the airport was a stranger, a recluse who had put in a rare public appearance when he was rebuked by the little man. The truth is that I'm very well acquainted this fellow. He shows up regularly with his sarcasm and a judgmental attitude. Much as I hate to admit it, these aren't occasional lapses. Something's wrong with me, and it needs fixing.

What's wrong, exactly?

Fixing what's wrong is what we do in the fourth step of the examen. Ignatius describes the fourth step very briefly: "The fourth point will be to ask pardon of God our Lord for my faults." He doesn't say how to go about this. It's not even clear exactly what he means by "faults." "Faults" is a mild word—it's easier for me to consider asking pardon for a "fault" than it is to admit to a "sin" or to root out a long-standing "character defect." I'm pretty sure Ignatius had something serious in mind when he wrote "fault."

The traditional word for it is "sin," which isn't very popular these days. I think that's the case not because people don't believe in evil or wrongdoing, but because of all the associations that go along with "sin." The term suggests sinners cowering before a vengeful, angry God, and it carries strong connotations of personal guilt. I like baseball metaphors. The God I'd learned about as a child was a demanding, rather chilly manager of a baseball team. I was out in the field, working hard to play a difficult game, and God was critically studying my performance. His patience was wearing thin as he watched me stumble around. Too many strikeouts, too many errors, and he'd put me on the bench. If it got bad enough, I'd be dismissed from the team.

There's another problem with sin. We usually understand sin to mean discrete acts that violate moral laws. A lie is a sin. Stealing money from your business partner is a sin. Adultery is a sin. True, but sinful actions aren't the real core of what's wrong with us. Lies, stealing, and adultery arise from deep disorders within. Our self-aware postmodern consciousness makes us exquisitely sensitive to the ways our behavior is shaped by bad parenting, addictions, betrayals, trauma, advertising, sibling rivalry, and unconscious striving for our father's approval. Our "sin problem" isn't the bad things we do that violate moral laws. The problem, as Joseph Tetlow, SJ, put

> Sinful actions aren't the real core of what's wrong with us. Lies, stealing, and adultery arise from deep disorders within.

it, is "the fact that I am from a dysfunctional family, work in a dysfunctional job, am surrounded by neurotics, with whom I fit perfectly."

This is what I realized when I thought about my outburst in the airport. On the flight to New York I gnawed at it obsessively. Why did it bother me so much? In a momentary fit of anger I had spoken nastily to a stranger, and I was sorry about that. I'll try not to do that again, with God's grace. Not a big deal—but it *was* a big deal. The big deal wasn't the angry outburst but the fact that I am the kind of guy who lashes out at people who bother me, especially people who are easy to bully, like janitors, technical support people in India, and high school kids running cash registers in retail stores.

Sin as failure

The problem is *me*. The behavior I regret is a manifestation of the real problem, a symptom of the disease. The best metaphor for sin is failure. We fall short of our own ideals. We don't thwart God so much as we thwart ourselves.

Years ago, I worked as a newspaper reporter. My paper investigated a county agency that seemed to be treating people in a high-handed and possibly unethical way. Several reporters worked on the story for months (I wasn't one of them). Their articles caused an uproar when they were published, and they had some good effects. The agency changed its procedures and some county employees were demoted and reassigned. But there were problems with the investigation. It came out that the reporters got some important facts wrong. They didn't give public officials a chance to tell their side of the story. Worst of all (at least to many), was that in the course of the investigation the reporters had lied about who they were and what they wanted.

I remember talking to one of the editors in the aftermath of this mess. He strongly believed in the ideals of journalism, and he was mortified at what his colleagues had done. He said, "It really hurts to publicly stand for high ideals and then fail to live up to them in such a public way."

This gets at the sense of failure that I associate with sin. We're intimately acquainted with failure, and it's very concrete. A pet project falls apart; we don't get the job; small children misbehave and adult children make poor decisions; a friend cuts off contact; marriages collapse. Someone once said that playing baseball is excellent training for life because baseball is all about failure. Players make three outs in every inning—a minimum of fifty-one outs in every game. Even the best hitters fail two-thirds of the time. That's the way life feels much of the time. Most things don't work the way I'd like them to. Much of the time I don't act the way I'd like to despite my high hopes, hard work, and fervent prayers.

How the examen helps

The examen helps us fix what's wrong by clarifying things. Failure is a pervasive, all-encompassing condition of life. Some of it is our responsibility and some of it isn't. Sometimes we accept responsibility when we shouldn't and shirk responsibility when we should accept it. As Joseph Tetlow puts it, "The examen frequently identifies sin at the source of an apparently faultless failure."

These are the situations in which we are quick to excuse ourselves: "payback" to someone who has wronged us, idle chatter that's really character assassination, angry tirades under the guise of "getting it off my chest." Careful reflection can even turn up a fault masquerading as virtue. Once I stood by silently while an acquaintance angrily insulted some friends of mine. I thought I was being prudent and restrained, but later I saw that I had been cowardly. I didn't want to risk unpleasantness (or worse) by doing the right thing and speaking up.

It works the other way too. We can mistakenly blame ourselves as well as excuse ourselves. We aren't responsible for other people's opinions and behavior. We can misread our motives and judge ourselves too harshly. Sometimes it's prudent, not cowardly, to hold your tongue. Sometimes you're wise, not lazy, to abandon a project that's draining your energy and isn't going anywhere.

Fr. Tetlow says that the examen helps us answer the question "Is my experience *my* sin, *a* sin, or sin *in* me?" When something goes wrong, this question helps to pinpoint exactly what the problem is.

For example, you're in a meeting and the boss asks why a deadline was missed. You lock horns with a colleague over it. The discussion gets a little heated. The boss intervenes, and gets the discussion back on track. At the end of the meeting you apologize for your part in the fracas.

Later in your examen you reflect on the scuffle. Was it *a* sin—a transgression of the moral law, something that's always wrong? Probably not. Raised voices and heated discussions per se aren't sins. Was it *my* sin—that is, did I cause something bad to happen? Perhaps. You may be responsible for the deadline being missed (harming the company) and wrongly blaming your co-worker (harming her). You probably acted wrongly by flying off the handle at the meeting. Was it sin *in* me—bad attitudes, faults, character defects? This is the really interesting question. Upon reflection you put the finger on some unattractive traits: envy of your colleague, sloth that's exposed by the missed deadline, and fear of public embarrassment.

This kind of reflection can help us make real progress in becoming the kind of person we want to be.

Love and scrupulosity

Facing up to what's wrong isn't fun; few of us rush to do this. Here are a couple of things to keep in mind when your enthusiasm for looking at failure and sin begin to fade.

First and foremost, this is a *response* to something God has initiated. This is true of the whole examen, but it's especially the case in the fourth step. God has invited us to look at what's wrong in our lives. We are not groveling before a hanging judge, pleading for mercy. We're not doing any of this under our own steam. God has invited us to do this, and the Holy Spirit guides us every step of the way. We're doing it only because we're in a personal and loving relationship with God.

Ignatius emphasized the reality of God's limitless love. He wrote in his diary, "God loves me more than I love myself." He was so secure in God's love that he once said that he would rather not feel consolation from God while he was examining his faults because the distress he felt spurred him on to make changes. I don't think I'd go that far; I'd like to feel consolation all the time! But I get Ignatius's point. God *will* respond to us. Ignatius says, "Ask pardon of God for our faults" in his brief instructions for step four. But that's only half the story. The second part is that God will respond with loving forgiveness.

Remember that the whole context of the examen is love. God is a generous giver of gifts—that's the image of God that makes the examen possible. If God is a fierce Divine Scorekeeper, it's very hard to admit faults and ask forgiveness. We're more inclined to hope that he wasn't looking and move on. But if God loves us more than we love ourselves, we're free to look clearly at what's wrong and do what's necessary to set things right.

> If God is a fierce Divine Scorekeeper, we find it hard to admit faults and ask forgiveness.

Anything can be taken to the extreme, and this is certainly the case with step four. Reflecting on faults can become excessive introspection. In fact, Ignatius himself is Exhibit A for morbid scrupulosity. Not long after his conversion he became obsessed by his sins. He practiced extreme penances and brought the same sins up repeatedly in the sacrament of confession. Finally his confessor ordered him to stop it and accept the fact that a loving God had forgiven him for his sins. Ignatius drew valuable lessons from this time in his life. He saw scrupulosity as a serious spiritual problem. From then on, in his own life and in the lives of those for whom he was a spiritual guide, Ignatius did not favor long fasts, mortification of the flesh, and other severe penitential practices. This is still generally true of Ignatius's followers today.

Scrupulosity can take milder forms. It's possible to spend too much time thinking about our faults—I'm inclined to do this myself. People who give me spiritual counsel have sometimes told me to stop thinking about my defects and faults and simply turn the whole problem over to God. (I'm even better at thinking about *other people's* faults, but that's a different problem.) Excessive introspection is self-centered. It can betray a subtle lack of confidence in God.

The point of it all is to grow in freedom. Sin hobbles our relationship with God, not because it's a black mark in the book kept by the Divine Scorekeeper, but because the lies, illusions, and self-serving excuses that cloud our minds make us less able to give and receive love. Looking at our sins and faults allows us to take responsibility for them. We can possess them; they no longer possess us. We become more and more able to give our whole selves to God, and to become the people God created us to be.

8

step five:
do something—but not
just anything

I don't have it all worked out, but I'm ready.
I want to try working with what I've got
instead of wishing I had something else.
—Mark Salzman, *Lying Awake*

In March of 1544, Ignatius had a big decision to make about how
the Jesuits would live their vow of poverty. Would it be strict or
flexible? How would poverty look in everyday terms as Jesuits
went about their work? A lot was stake, and Jesuits had different
ideas about it. It was time to make a decision, and because Ignatius
was the Superior General of the order, it was his call.

Ignatius undertook a formal and very thorough discernment
process to seek God's will in the matter. What's of interest here is
what happened at the end. After he had made up his mind what to
do, Ignatius was assaulted by doubts. He thought he should reopen
the question. He worried that he might have completely misread
the leading of the Holy Spirit. At the very least, he thought he
should look for more signs confirming the decision, even though
he earlier thought that God had given many signs of confirmation.

What Ignatius did was to expel these doubts from his mind and move ahead with what he thought God wanted. He wrote: "I began to strive to move my heart toward what was pleasing to God."

Ignatius *did* something, but the main thing he did was to look back on what he had experienced of Christ in the days and weeks of his discernment prayer. He strove to move his heart toward what God wanted. His heart wasn't quite where he wanted it to be; Ignatius didn't have the certainty he wanted. He feared making the wrong decision about how the Jesuits should live in poverty. But he pushed ahead anyway in the assurance that God had shown him what he needed to know.

What will I do today?

The question, "What will I do today?" is the heart of the fifth step of the examen. In this last part of the examen we resolve to act rightly in the day ahead. The basis for this decision is what we have experienced of Christ in the hours of the immediate past. We've seen God at work, and we've reflected on what's gone wrong and what could be improved. There are many things we *could* do, and it's almost always the case that we'd like some more clarity about what we *should* do. Nevertheless we decide to take action, based on our experience of God in the day we've just lived. The important thing is "to move my heart toward what was pleasing to God."

We want to be doers. The Nike motto "Just *Do* It!" is a great brand slogan because it taps into deep impulses and urges. Stop talking—*act*. Stop dreaming—*do* something to realize your dreams. Do *something* instead of thinking and dithering. For people paralyzed by procrastination, this can often be the right thing to do. Start the engines and get the ship moving in the water; worry about steering it later. But "just do it" isn't exactly the motive that should carry us through the last step of the examen. The goal is to grow closer to Christ, not to act for the sake of acting.

> The goal is to grow closer to Christ, not to act for the sake of acting.

We need to act wisely, as God would have us act. The question to ask yourself is "What will I do *today*?" I have a long to-do list written on a sheet of paper that lies next to my keyboard. I work in two different offices, and I carry the list around with me. (I haven't put it in my phone yet—that's one of the items on the list.) My list is a mixture of personal and professional tasks, small errands and big projects, the urgent and the postponable, the practical and the dreamy. This list is *the future*. Most days I go through the list and select the tasks that I will do *today*. That's what we do in the fifth step of the daily examen. We narrow things down. The future becomes today.

Today isn't going to be what you expect. Your boss will give you a new project; people who have promised to get back to you won't do it; someone you haven't heard from in months will call or drop in; you'll open an email and discover that you have to stop what you're doing and tend to a problem immediately; your spouse will be delayed at work, disrupting dinner and the evening plans; your sister will call, asking for a big favor. You can't control this pandemonium, but you do have influence over it. There are some steps you can take to get more closely aligned to Christ, who is in it all.

The Jesuit spiritual director George Aschenbrenner calls this step of the examen "hopeful resolution for the future." He emphasizes "hopeful." Aschenbrenner reminds us to be sure to examine our feelings at this stage of the examen and to always be honest in our relationship with God. Hopeful resolution for the future is something that occurs in our hearts. We've become sensitive to the ebb and flow of consolation and desolation in the course of praying the examen. Here at the end, when we're looking to do things differently tomorrow, our hearts are the first place to look for guidance.

One thing at a time

"One day at a time" is a motto for people recovering from addictive behaviors in twelve-step programs. "One thing at a time" is a good motto for people trying to get better in tune with Christ through the daily examen.

What might that one thing be? It depends, obviously. It depends on what God has been doing in your life. It depends on your sense of what needs changing, and on what the Holy Spirit has been leading you to pay attention to. You might work on the same problem for a while. More likely, the one thing that you resolve to do at the end of the examen will change frequently. The examen is a personal discernment of the state of a relationship. The relationship with God is a dynamic one; new people, events, challenges, and opportunities will constantly arise.

Quite often I will ask, "Where do I need God most tomorrow?" My feelings usually supply the answer. I'm worried (deadline, important meeting, presentation coming up); flummoxed (it looks like we can't afford the vacation we planned); upset (my friend is in trouble. What can I do?); sad (I'm going to a wake tonight). I ask God to give me what I will need to deal with the situation at hand.

Much of the time the one thing is a small thing. Today, you're not going to launch a comprehensive plan to repair a troubled family relationship. You *might* do something small, like inviting a reclusive relative out for a cup of coffee, or sending her a "thinking of you" card. I'm trying to change a habit of ignoring non-urgent tedious and unpleasant jobs I have to do. Some days I'll take one of those postponable items on my list and do it. I take a garbage bag full of old files to the shredder. I wash windows. I scrape the old flaking paint on the garage. I balance checkbooks. I back up my computer.

"Small thing" doesn't mean "easy thing." I was appalled and ashamed after my outburst in the airport. My arrogance and anger seemed like a very big problem, a firmly rooted part of *me*. I was discouraged and didn't know how to tackle it.

The small thing I did was to tell my wife Susan about it. Even though she knows all about this side of me, I didn't look forward to telling her about this latest flare-up. But the conversation went very well and she gave me some helpful insights. Soon I told some other people about it. Talking about the problem took some of the sting out of it. I learned how to be alert to impending trouble. I asked God to change me.

About a year later, I was on the speakerphone in my home office talking to a technician at a web hosting company about a problem with my account. I didn't like the way the guy was talking to me. He was blaming me for a problem that I was sure was theirs. He was irked and impatient with me. Inwardly, I climbed up on my high horse and rehearsed a speech about what a good customer I had been and how I deserved better treatment than this and who did he think he was, anyway, talking to me like that. But outwardly I took a deep breath, lowered my voice, chose my words carefully, and continued to discuss the problem, which was resolved after a while. (Sure enough, I *had* done something careless to mess up my account.)

My wife overheard the speakerphone conversation; she complimented me on the way I had handled it. "You've changed," she said. Not entirely, I thought. My behavior was better, but the same arrogant, angry impulses surged up inside when I was provoked. They lingered too. (OK, it was my fault, but he still shouldn't have talked to me that way.) But I made progress, and it came mostly in small steps—admitting the problem instead of pushing it aside, talking about it, praying about it. As for the angry impulses— God will have to change that.

Mysterious words about deeds

A Jesuit ministry I'm part of gave out some gifts to its employees and friends at a social get-together. One was a card with a picture of Ignatius Loyola on one side and one of his most famous sayings on the other. I've already mentioned it: "Love ought to manifest itself in deeds rather than in words." It's a deep thought because it seems both profoundly true and subtly enigmatic. It's true: what you *do* matters most. It matters more than what you say, especially when you're in a relationship with someone. But Ignatius's comment is also mysterious. Words matter too. Loving words and loving deeds go together. Shouldn't it be both deeds *and* words, not deeds *rather* than words?

I think there's a touch of hyperbole in Ignatius's saying; I think he said it the way he did in order to guard against something. He didn't want prayer to become an end in itself. Prayer is essential, but prayer leads to deeds—to change, to work, to concrete acts of love. There's a chronic temptation to rest contentedly in the prayer and neglect the deeds. On the mount of Transfiguration the apostles wanted to build tents for Moses and Elijah to prolong the vision of glory that they enjoyed so much. At the Ascension the disciples mourned the departed Jesus until the angel came and rebuked them for gaping at the sky. There was work to be done!

So too with examen prayer. Finding God in everyday life is such a pleasant experience that we can forget that there's work to be done. God loves us just the way we are, but this doesn't mean that God *approves* everything about us. He accepts us *despite* many things. I think that God's acceptance of us "just as we are" is something like that. It's unconditional love without blanket approval.

I also think that God's love for us "just as we are" means loving us in our relationships. We're not isolated individuals in the eyes of God. "Just as you are" means you as a spouse, parent, son or daughter, friend, colleague, parishioner, citizen, volunteer, and neighbor. Joseph Tetlow puts it beautifully: "God accepts me not as a lone candle in a vast dark space, but like a fine voice in a choir making a personal contribution to the song we all sing."

How are these relationships going? Are you neglecting any of them? A friend of mine often takes out his phone during his examen and scrolls through the names in the contact list, asking the Holy Spirit to show him relationships that need attention. The one thing you resolve to do today might be to call an old friend you haven't talked to in a long time. Or you might reach out to that colleague or family member with whom you've felt tense and awkward lately.

It's up to God

Ignatius worded the fifth point of the examen carefully: "The fifth point will be to resolve to amend with the grace of God" (43). In the examen, we resolve to amend. The actual amending—the deed—comes later. It may not come easily; it may not come at all. The action comes *with the grace of God*. All we can do is make up our minds to try.

Five hundred years after Ignatius wrote the *Spiritual Exercises*, an alcoholic named Bill Wilson sat down at his kitchen table in New York City and wrote down the 12 Steps of Alcoholics Anonymous. Step 6 is "Were entirely ready to have God remove all these defects of character." An alcoholic reaches Step 6 after identifying the defects of character that need fixing. Step 6 doesn't say "*took steps* to remove all these defects of character" or even "*decided* to remove all these defects of character. It simply says "*were entirely ready*" to have God do it.

That's because we can't do these things on our own. All we can do is *resolve* to make changes, to become ready to have *God* do it. You can decide to make the appointment you've been putting off and the phone call you've been dreading. You can resolve to help your teenager with her math homework this evening without getting angry. You can make up your mind to do something to get your family finances in better order. But the power to do these things isn't yours—it's God's. God gives you the grace to do the deed, and when you do it, the outcome is up to God too.

the real-time examen

Father Urban had preached a great many
thrilling sermons on saints who had really
asked for the martyr's crown, but he believed
that there were others from whose lives we
might learn more that would serve us better
in the daily round. What of those who had
remained on the scene and got on with the
job? The work of the Church, after all, had
to be done for the most part by the living.
There was too much emphasis on dying for
the faith. How about living for the faith?

—J. F. Powers, *Morte D'Urban*

My wife and I were having dinner with another couple, old friends
of ours, when the conversation turned, somewhat surprisingly, to
prayer. My friend Dave runs a good-sized company. Lately, some
unusual things had been happening. He would be chairing a
stressful meeting or listening to one of his managers talk about
a knotty problem and he would suddenly become detached from
the situation. He'd become aware of God's presence. He'd say to
himself something like, "that's interesting, God is in that idea."
Or, if the situation seemed confused and tiresome, he'd think
"Please come God. I'm going to wait until you show up."

Dave described the kind of reflection that goes on in the examen prayer, only he was doing it in real time, not in a fifteen-minute block of time set aside at the beginning or end of the day. In fact, this is the goal of the daily examen. Our aim is to be sensitive to God all the time. The daily examen is a training exercise designed to cultivate a reflective habit of mind that makes us sensitive to God everywhere and at all times. When that happens, we can truly say that the examen changes everything.

A contemplative in action

Ignatius seems to have been a man who achieved this state of constant discerning awareness. Jerome Nadal, perhaps his closest associate, wrote that Ignatius was able "to see and contemplate in all things, actions, and conversations the presence of God and the love of spiritual things, to remain a contemplative in action."

How I would love to be a "contemplative in action" like Ignatius! It would solve the "prayer problem"—the separation of prayer from life. It would solve the "Christian problem"—the question of what is distinctive in everyday terms about being a follower of Jesus Christ. The answer is to be aware of God all the time. Contemplation and action are the two poles on the spiritual axis. Sometimes we pray; the rest of the time we work. Not so, said Ignatius. He brought contemplation and action together, and the tool he used to join them is the reflective awareness of God that is at the heart of the examen. A perfect example of a contemplative in action is my friend Dave, looking for God's presence in a meeting about his company's inventory problems.

Another way to put it is that the goal of the examen is to help us "find God in all things." This is another Ignatian catchphrase that describes something I find very appealing. Finding God in all things doesn't mean that all things are divine. That's pantheism, and Christians believe that the Creator is distinct from the creation. What the phrase means is that "all things" is where we find God. Our work, our relationships, the created world—God is at work in all of them. We don't find him only in special places like church or at special times like morning prayer. The examen cultivates a constant discerning awareness of God's presence at all times—even the busiest, most stressful, and tedious times.

The real-time examen is the end of the examen—in both senses of "end." It's the end as the goal: the point is to perceive God all the time, not just for fifteen minutes a day. It's also the end of thinking of the examen as a scheduled prayer done in five steps at a certain time every day. An examen can be done anywhere—when we're stuck in traffic, eating lunch, walking to class, standing in line, or sitting in meetings. It's always a good idea to set aside time to review the day in the presence of the Holy Spirit, but a discerning sensitivity to God is something we can possess all the time.

> An examen can be done anywhere— when we're stuck in traffic, eating lunch, walking to class, standing in line, or sitting in meetings.

The examen is not an end in itself

Constant awareness of God—what more could we want from a spiritual practice? But remember Ignatius's saying that love should be expressed in deeds rather than words. The thankful reflection brought about by practicing the examen is not an end in itself, a state of Zen-like bliss. We want to be aware of what God is doing in our lives so that we can respond to God better. The question we want answered is: What shall we *do*?

Ignatius didn't invent the examen, and he was hardly the first Christian thinker to emphasize the importance of responding to God by actively working in the world. But one of his great accomplishments was to put prayer, action, and spiritual growth in a context that explains why we do these things. He gave a compelling "big picture," a worldview that has made sense to many people over the past five centuries.

Ignatius laid out his big picture in a short passage at the beginning of the *Spiritual Exercises* called "The First Principle and Foundation" (23). The first sentence answers the question, "Why are we here?" "Man is created to praise, reverence, and serve God our Lord, and by this means to save his soul." The next two sentences specify how this is to happen:

> The other things on the face of the earth are created
> for man to help him in attaining the end for which
> he is created. Hence, man is to make use of them
> in as far as they help him in the attainment of his
> end, and he must rid himself of them in as far as
> they prove a hindrance to him.

Here is the great challenge of life: to choose the good ("make use of them in as far as they help him in the attainment of his end") and avoid the bad ("rid himself of them in as far as they prove a hindrance to him"). "Them" is "the other things on the face of the earth," in other words, everything—the work we do, the people in our lives, our responsibilities, our ambitions and hopes and disappointments, the opportunities and misfortunes that come our way, the way we interact with the institutions of human society. All of it is meaningful. Nothing is so small, so fleeting, so distasteful, or so awful that it's excluded from the drama of life.

In the Ignatian big picture, how we choose is just about the most important thing we do. The First Principle and Foundation sets forth some of the necessary conditions for making good choices.

> Therefore we must make ourselves indifferent to all created things, as far as we are allowed free choice and are not under any prohibition. Consequently . . . we should not prefer health to sickness, riches to poverty, honor to dishonor, a long life to a short life. The same holds for all other things.
>
> Our one desire and choice should be what is more conducive to the end for which we are created.

We shouldn't care whether we die young, get sick, or live in poverty? That's not what Ignatius means. He's saying that we shouldn't care about our health or our financial security or our reputation or anything else so much that these things determine our choices. We're to be "indifferent" to them—that is, free from attachments to them. Only by being detached from created things can we make good choices about them, so that we can achieve the end for which we are created.

That's the big picture. We're here to love and serve God. The things in the world help and hinder us in this task. We must make good choices, and to choose well we must be free. The examen is a tool we use all along the way—to find God in our lives, to discover what needs to be done, to reflect on our actions and motives, and to make good choices.

That, in a nutshell, is what Ignatian spirituality is all about. Ignatius brought contemplation and action together, but the senior partner in the alliance is action. In the Ignatian scheme of things, we love and serve God by being joined with Christ in the work of saving and healing the world. The end of the examen is action—responding to God more faithfully, discerning our part in Christ's mission, and making good decisions about how to fulfill it.

Surprise me

Sometimes prayer is easy. Much of the time it's not. You're going to run into difficulties if you try to make the examen prayer a regular habit. Here's a sampling of complaints, from people I know or know about.

Carrie, a translator: "It seems so artificial. I don't like going down a five-step checklist when I pray."

Charlie, a hospital administrator: "It depressed me. I didn't like thinking about all the things that went wrong in my day, especially the things that had *I* had done wrong."

Isabella, a college student: "It's hard for me to believe that I can find God in the trivial and stupid stuff that goes on in my day."

Gene, a salesman: "I just got bored with it."

I'd like to say that these problems are easily solved: that if you stick with it, the examen won't seem artificial; that if you pay closer attention, it won't be boring; that if you get your mind off yourself, you won't be depressed; that if you persist, you'll realize that God really is in the stuff you do every day. But I can't say that. Problems crop up again and again in a life of prayer.

All the usual advice about prayer applies here: set a regular time for prayer and stick to it; be patient when little seems to be happening; do more listening than speaking; be attentive. If you don't do these things, the daily examen will become the weekly examen, then the occasional examen. The idea that spiritual growth involves discomfort shouldn't come as a surprise to anyone who is reading this book. Of all people, we Christians should know better than to think that prayer is bliss. We have the constant example of Jesus Christ to remind us that the path to freedom lies through suffering.

There's one more thing you can do to keep the examen fresh: let yourself be surprised. The examen is the prayer of surprises. Some surprises are unpleasant (at least initially) but most are not. You will find God in places where you never thought to look.

Once in my examen I recalled a long and inconclusive meeting I had just been part of. It frustrated me, and I grumbled to God about it. Then a different thought popped into my head: It had been a privilege to be in that meeting. The work I do is good work. My colleagues are gifted and dedicated people. Through the meeting that I found so frustrating, I was participating in Christ's mission to save and heal the world. This line of thinking surprised me. Where did it come from? It had to have come from God. The surprises continued. My next thought was a question: How could I have participated better in that meeting? Since honest self-appraisal isn't my usual style, I figured that this thought came from God too.

The poet Mary Karr says this about hearing God: "I don't mean the voice of Charlton Heston playing Moses booming from on high, but reversals of attitude so contrary to my typical thought—so solidly true—as to seem divinely external." We know it's God's voice because it's *different*. It's a surprise.

And perhaps we can surprise God. One of my favorite novels is *Mariette in Ecstasy* by Ron Hansen, a story about a young nun who has mystical visions. The novel ends with these words, from a letter Mariette writes to a friend long after she has left the community.

> And Christ still sends me roses. We try to be formed
> and held and kept by him, but instead he offers us
> freedom. And now when I try to know his will, his
> kindness floods me, his great love overwhelms me,
> and I hear him whisper, Surprise me.

Can we surprise God? Probably not in some ultimate metaphysical sense; God knows all in his dwelling place in eternity. But in our daily relationship with Jesus, I wouldn't dismiss the idea out of hand. We crave certainty; "instead he offers us freedom." This opens the door to surprise. Even if we don't surprise God, we can surprise ourselves.

now it's your turn

Enough from me. It's time for you to stop reading about the examen and start praying it yourself. I'm not going to say that you *should* pray this way. I'm not a big fan of "shoulds" in matters of personal prayer (and in most other matters too). I much prefer the pragmatic Ignatian principle: "whatever works." Ignatius Loyola esteemed the examen highly. He thought it had many benefits, and he urged people to pray it. But he was a practical man who didn't let rules and "shoulds" get in the way. If you are content with your experience of prayer, by all means stick with it. The examen isn't the only way to pray.

But the examen is a way that everyone can pray, and if you're looking for a change or a boost or some encouragement, you might give it a try. Try it for at least a month—at least long enough for the novelty to wear off. You want to get comfortable enough so that the examen doesn't seem artificial. Choose a regular time to pray it, usually at the beginning or end of the day. Here are the steps of the prayer:

1. **Pray for light.**
   Begin by asking God for the grace to pray, to see, and to understand.

2. **Give thanks.**
   Look at your day in a spirit of gratitude. Everything is a gift from God.

3. **Review the day.**
   Guided by the Holy Spirit, look back on your day. Pay attention to your experience. Look for God in it.

4. **Look at what's wrong.**
   Face up to failures and shortcomings. Ask forgiveness for your faults. Ask God to show you ways to improve.

5. **Resolve what to do in the day to come.**
   Where do you need God today? What can you do today?

Don't limit the examen to a special fifteen- or twenty-minute block of time. You can reflect on God's presence whenever you have some down time. And if you feel the urge to look for God while you're actively engaged in work or with other people, by all means give into it. God is surely there.

a note on language, resources, and sources

Pronouns for God

In many places in this book I refer to God as "he" and "him." I do this reluctantly as the "least bad" choice. I think it is very important to think of God as a personal being with whom we have a personal relationship. I especially want to convey this in a book about the most personal of personal prayers. Using a personal pronoun to refer to God strengthens the idea of a personal relationship. The stylistic alternative available in the English language is to avoid all personal pronouns in reference to God. I think this makes God seem less personal. By referring to God as "he" I'm not suggesting that God is male. I'm trying to say that God is near.

Resources

To learn more about the examen, look at the articles, videos, podcasts, and handouts available in the Daily Examen section of the website IgnatianSpirituality.com. Start with Dennis Hamm's article "Rummaging for God: Praying Backwards through Your Day" and go on from there.

IgnatianSpirituality.com is also a good place to learn more about Ignatian spirituality more broadly. The site has sections on the *Spiritual Exercises*, Ignatian retreats, prayer, discernment, and making good decisions.

For further reading about Ignatian spirituality, I'd start with *The Jesuit Guide to (Almost) Everything* by James Martin, SJ. I'd also recommend these books:

What Is Ignatian Spirituality? by David L. Fleming, SJ
Inner Compass by Margaret Silf
Contemplatives in Action by William Barry, SJ, and Robert Doherty, SJ
The Ignatian Workout by Tim Muldoon
Friendship with God by William Barry, SJ
Making Choices in Christ by Joseph Tetlow, SJ

Sources

My approach to the examen has been shaped by the work of George Aschenbrenner, SJ, and Joseph Tetlow, SJ. Fr. Aschenbrenner's 1972 article "Consciousness Examen" transformed the way Jesuits approached the prayer. All of my quotations of Fr. Aschenbrenner in this book have been taken from this article. A slightly abridged version of it can be found in the Daily Examen section of IgnatianSpirituality.com.

Three important papers by Fr. Tetlow deeply influenced my thinking about the examen. They are "The Most Postmodern Prayer," "An Examen: The Person in Relationships," and "The Examen of Particulars." All three have been published by the Institute of Jesuit Sources at Boston College. The latter two were collected in the book *Sharing the Spiritual Exercises of St. Ignatius*, edited by David L. Fleming SJ. All of my quotes from Fr. Tetlow are from these papers.

Additional Notes on Sources

Chapter 5, page 34: Ignatius's remarks about ingratitude and receiving God's gifts are cited in *The Examen Prayer* by Timothy M. Gallagher, OSV (New York: Crossroad, 2006).

Chapter 6, page 41: Walter Burghardt, SJ, from *Contemplation: A Long Loving Look at the Real*. http://www.theyardleygroup.com/Burghardt_-_Contemplation_a_long_loving.pdf.

Chapter 8, pages 61–2: Ignatius's discernment in March, 1544 is described by Gallagher in *The Examen Prayer*. Quotations are taken from Gallagher.

Chapter 9, page 72: Jerome Nadal on Ignatius as a contemplative in action from Joseph de Guibert, *The Jesuits: Their Spiritual Doctrine and Practice* (Chicago: Loyola University Press, 1964).

Chapter 9, page 78: Mary Karr on hearing God from *Lit: A Memoir* (New York: Harper, 2009).